# Gardeners' Guide to Growing Green Beans in the Vegetable Garden

## The Green Bean Book – Growing Bush, Pole Beans For Beginning Gardeners

## Gardener's Guide to Growing Your Vegetable Garden – Book II

# Paul R. Wonning

Gardeners' Guide to Growing Green Beans in the Vegetable Garden

Published By Paul R. Wonning
Copyright 2016 by Paul R. Wonning
Print Edition

paulwonning@gmail.com

If you would like email notification of when new Mossy Feet books become available email the author for inclusion in the subscription list.

Join Me on Facebook

Search Mossy Feet Books

Find them on www.mossyfeetbooks.com

**Mossy Feet Books**

## Description

String beans, bush beans, pole beans, they are all the same species and have similar needs in the garden.

*Gardeners' Guide to Growing Green Beans in the Vegetable Garden* covers all the green beans. It is an excellent vegetable garden guide for the garden beginner as well as the veteran gardener.

Gardeners will find sections on pole beans, dry beans, bush beans and half runner beans. Planting, culture, harvest and storage of all the different types of beans is covered as well.

The guide covers heirloom beans as well, and *Gardeners' Guide to Growing Green Beans in the Vegetable Garden* contains a list of seed sources as well. It will please gardeners to find our extensive list of seed catalogs included as well. This updated catalog includes some new seed catalog finds.

The garden vegetable series *Gardeners' Guide to Growing Your Vegetable* Garden includes this book. This exciting new series of vegetable gardening books will include twenty vegetables. These are the most common ones grown in the home vegetable garden. The books will all include complete growing, culture, botanical, harvesting and storage information. Great for veteran or beginning gardeners the series is written for gardeners by a gardener.

## Table of Contents

**Common Name:**

Garden Bean, Snap bean, green bean, string bean

Snap bean refers to the "snap" sound the bean makes when cooks break the bean in half. Many call them string beans because of the "string" of skin that runs along the seam of the bean that resembles a thread when removed. Since people consume these beans unripe with the seed still in the pod, they call them "green beans." The author refers to them as a whole in this book as garden beans because both the green and dry versions of beans are included in this volume.

**Botanical Name:**

Phaseolus vulgaris

The genus name is the Greek name for a type of bean. Vulgaris is Latin for common.

**Family:**

Leguminosae, Fabaceae

Fabaceae is a new name fixed by botanists that derives from the Latin word "bean." Leguminosae is an older name, still used, which is a Latin term that refers to the fruit.

The Fabaceae family is a large family that consists of annual, perennial plants, trees, vines and herbs. It is the third largest plant family with 630 genera and over one8,860 species. Many of the members of this family have great economic importance. These include peas, beans, soybeans, licorice, alfalfa and clover. Most members of this family have a fruit that botanists refer to as a legume. This seeds develop inside a pod that has two seams. Several seeds usually inhabit each pod. Most members of this family also host bacteria called rhizobia in nodules on their roots. These bacteria have the important function of taking nitrogen from the air and converting it to a form that most plants can use. This trait makes legumes an important part of a gardeners plant rotation. These bacteria convert more nitrogen than their hosts can use. The remainder of the nitrogen stays in the soil after the plant has completed its life cycle, making it available to other plants.

**Sun:**

Full sun

At least six to eight hours of sun per day

**Soil:**

Rich, well drained slightly acidic pH of about 6.0 to 6.2. They dont need nitrogen fertilizer because they can fix their own from the atmosphere

## Hardiness Zone:

Garden beans are tropical in origin and are quite sensitive to cold and frost. Plant them only after the soil has warmed and danger of frost has passed. Planting too early will result in rotted seeds, not early beans.

Back to Garden Bean Index

## Origins:

Snap beans originated in the hot tropics, mostly Central and South America, Indian and China. Spanish conquistadores carried the garden bean to Europe in one597. The American Indians cultivated snap beans, growing them in the same mounds with corn and squash, the famed "three sisters" growing system. The Amerindians would not have eaten these beans green. Instead, they would have let them mature and harvested them as dry beans.

Back to Garden Bean Index

**Propagation:**

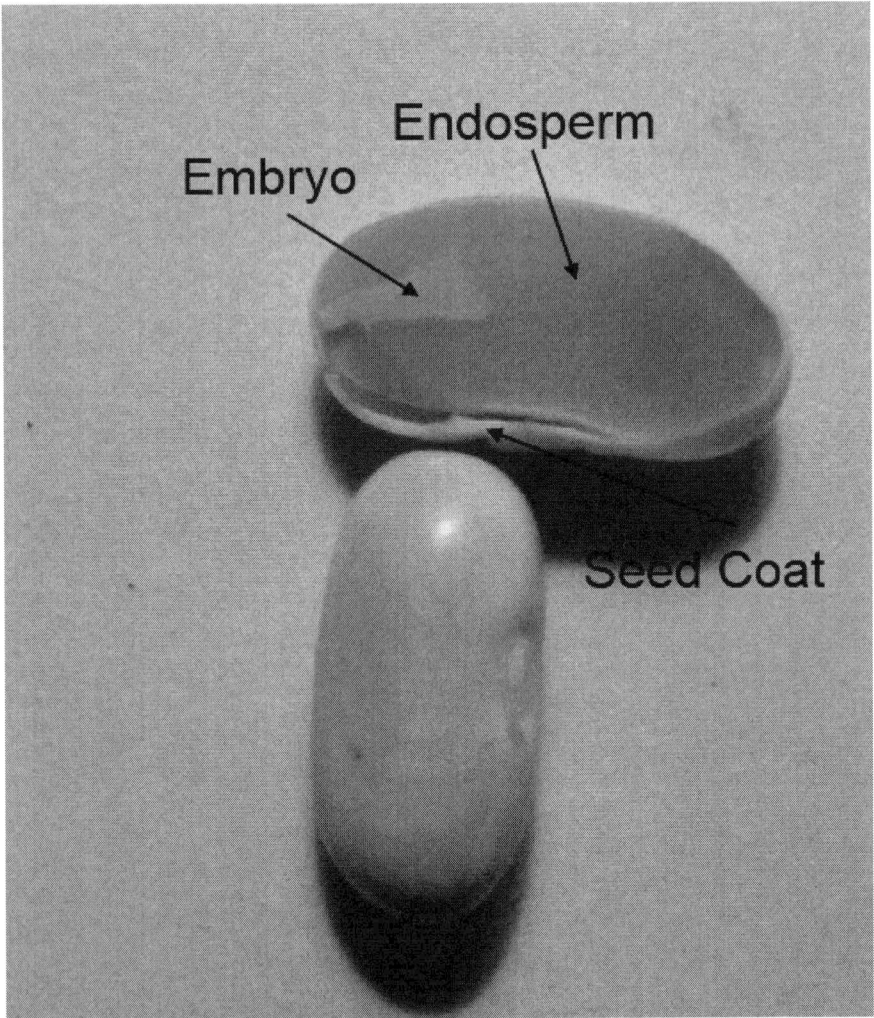

**Seed**

Plant snap beans in the garden after all danger of frost have past. They will take seven to ten days to germinate when the soil temperature has reached 65 - 70 degrees. Plant the seeds one and a half to two inches deep and about six inches apart in the row. Rows separation depends upon you gardening method. If you hand cultivate or grow in raised beds plant the seeds about six inches apart. If planting in rows, make sure the row width accommodates your garden tiller or other machine. Pole beans will need some sort of trellis system.

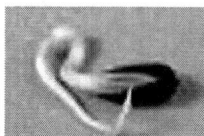

You can plant beans early in a hot bed or greenhouse. Plant them in a three inch pot three to four weeks before frost and set the seedlings in the garden after all danger of frost has passed. Use a big enough pot so you dont have to transplant the seedlings into a bigger one, as bean seedlings dont transplant well.

**Plant Height, Spread, Spacing:**

Plant Height:

Bush - Twelve to twenty four inches

Half Runner - Twenty to thirty six inches

Pole - Six to fifteen feet

Spread:

Bush - Twelve to fifteen inches

Half Runner - Twelve to fifteen inches

Pole - Twelve to fifteen inches

Spacing:

Bush - Two to six inches apart in rows twenty-four to thirty inches apart

Half Runner - Four to eight inches in rows twenty four to thirty six inches apart

Pole - Four to eight inches in rows twenty four to thirty six inches apart

## Flower Color, Description and Fragrance:

The half-inch flowers are white, pink or yellow, most commonly white. They have both male and female parts and are self-fertile.

## Plant Description:

Garden bean species all have green or purple alternate leaves. The leaves divide into three oval leaflets with smooth edges. Plant height is variable; bush varieties are erect and grow to twenty-four inches tall. Vining varieties are twining in habit and can grow to ninety-six inches tall. Half runners have a growing habit half way between bush and vining types and can grow to thirty-six inches.

## Nitrogen-fixing ability

Peas, and other legumes garden plants like beans, have the ability to take nitrogen in the atmosphere and fix it in the soil in which they grow. The plants do this by using bacteria located in nodules on the plants roots. This symbiotic relationship is beneficial to both the legumes and the bacteria. The bacteria take nitrogen from the oxygen and, by a complex chemical process, convert it to ammonia. Ammonia is nitrogen in a form that plants can use it. The plants pay the bacteria back by supplying sugars to the bacteria that it needs to survive. The bacteria are a special kind called Rhizobium bacteria. The bacteria are specific to the plant, thus the Rhizobium bacteria that peas need are a different species from the ones that beans require. This bacteria is usually present in garden soil.

## Deficiencies of Rhizobium

If the type of legume you are planting has not been planted in the garden before, if it is a new plot or you have not planted the plant before it is possible that these bacteria are not present. Using chemical fertilizers or pesticides can also kill the bacteria. To ensure that the bacteria are present, you may coat the seed with an innoculant that contains the correct bacteria at seed planting time. The innoculant sold in garden stores and mail order seed supply companies usually contain a mix of bacteria that will inoculate most garden crops. These inoculants are inexpensive. The inoculants will have an expiration date and must be stored properly for them to survive. The species needed for most garden crops are:

Common Beans - R. leguminosarum bv. phaseoli

Field or Garden Peas - R. leguminosarum bv. viciae

Peanut - Bradyrhizobium sp.

Chickpeas - Mesorhizobium sp.

Soybeans - Bradyrhizobium japonicum

To use, moisten the seed and dust the innoculant over it. mix it in well and plant immediately. You can also sprinkle the innoculant into the soil where you are planting the seeds. Work it in well. Some seeds are pre-inoculated, so check the seed packet, which will state it on the package if it is. Store unused innoculant in a sealed plastic bag in an area with consistent temperatures. A refrigerator will work. Properly stored, the innoculant should keep for a year.

temperatures. A refrigerator will work. Properly stored, the innoculant should keep for a year.

Legume crops like peas and beans will fix more nitrogen in the soil than they need. This nitrogen is available for future crops grown in the garden and can reduce fertilizer for other vegetables. Farmers have taken advantage of this nitrogen fixing ability for generations by rotating legume crops with other field crops.

**Garden Culture:**

After planting, bush beans will need little care other than to check for insect pests or disease every few days. Pole beans will need some sort of support to climb. An extra feeding of manure, compost or diluted liquid fertilizer can benefit beans. Apply it about halfway through the growing season.

**Garden Culture:**

After planting, bush beans will need little care other than to check for insect pests or disease every few days. Pole beans will need some sort of support to climb. An extra feeding of manure, compost or diluted liquid fertilizer can benefit beans. Apply it about halfway through the growing season.

## Pollination:

Honeybees, bumble bees and carpenter bees pollinate them. Bumble and carpenter bees appear to be the most efficient. Beans can self-pollinate and hand pollination is possible. Use a small brush to collect pollen off the anther onto the pistil. You can use a paintbrush; make up brush or cotton swab.

## Problems:

### Mexican Bean Beetles

This member of the ladybug family can devastate a planting of beans quickly. The insects resemble ladybugs, but are yellow or coppery brown and will have about sixteen black or brown spots. The larvae are yellow and about one quarter to one half inch long. The larvae have a spiky appearance and attach themselves to the leaves. The eggs will be on the underside of the leaves. These are orange and appear in large groups. Few predators feed on these bugs because they excrete an unpleasant smelling substance. Heavy infestations will strip the leaves, eventually killing the plant.

Controls:

Adults can over winter in plant debris, so it is important to clean the garden in the fall. Ladybugs, green lacewing and minute pirate bugs are all predators of both the egg and young larvae of the beetle. Neem, insecticidal soap will also control them. Make sure to spray both top and bottom of the leaves. Hand picking small infestations is feasible. Make sure to inspect the underside of the leaves and remove the eggs. Diatomaceous earth is also an effective control.

## Slugs

These creatures like damp, dark conditions. They will feed on any part of the plant that touches the ground. Use slug traps or diatomaceous earth to control. Pick up anything the slugs might shelter under like boards, large rocks.

## Japanese beetles

These insects, if present, are hard to control as few insecticides are effective against them. The insects are bi-color, with brown wings and a green head. They are about one-half inch long and feed on a wide variety of plants, including beans. Row covers can exclude them from landing and eating. Studies have shown that traps may merely attract them to the plant, but not necessarily lure them into the trap. They may just land and feed on surrounding plants. The only effective control is to treat the lawn with milky spore disease, which will kill the grubs. This will kill them, but if neighbors do not use the product, the beetles will still be a pest. One effective method for control is hand picking.

## Aphids

Most aphids are green and small, but they can be other colors. They suck the plant juices from both leaves and stems, weakening it. They will appear on the stems and underside of the leaves. Insecticidal soap is a good control. Crushing the insects with the fingers is effective for small infestations. Inspect the plants frequently for them as a small infestation can turn into a large infestation quickly. Ants spread them, as they use the honeydew that they excrete as a food source. Controlling ants will sometimes control the aphids.

## Alternaria

This fungal disease begins as a small brown or yellow spot. The spot will expand, forming concentric rings. When the rings on a leaf join, the leaf will fall off. There are no controls once the disease starts. Fungicides may help. Read the label. The best controls are cultural. Some weeds can be alternate hosts, so keep the garden weed free. Clean up the garden in the fall, as the fungus can over winter in dead plant material. Use certified seed, as seeds can carry the disease.

## Mosaic disease

The bean mosaic diseases cause plants to turn a yellowish green and produce few or no pods. The leaves on infected plants are a mottled yellow and are usually irregularly shaped. The only satisfactory control for these diseases is to use mosaic-resistant bean varieties.

## Angular leaf spot - bacterial bean blight

Bacterial bean blight is a disease that will cause brown spots that quickly grow, killing the leaf. Warm, wet weather encourages the disease. Control bacterial blight by planting disease-free seed. Avoid contact with wet bean plants and remove all bean debris from the garden. The pathogens can survive in infected debris and are seed-borne. Disease management recommendations rely upon crop rotation, sanitation, planting treated certified seed. Choose resistant varies. Good culture avoids stress that makes plants susceptible. Once started on a plant, there is no control. Remove the infected plants and destroy them to prevent the spread.

## Seed rot

Do not plant in cold, moist soils.

## Medicinal uses Health Benefits:

Beans, both dry and green, provide many health benefits when consumed. They are a major source of fiber and protein as well as complex carbohydrates. Humans have used beans, especially dry beans, as a food source since ancient times. Nutritionists consider beans to be nutrient dense. This means that they pack many nutrients compared to their calories. Consuming beans frequently can be good for overall health. Evidence points to a longer life for people that consume beans frequently. Three cups of dry beans per week can help reduce chronic diseases such as obesity, cancer, diabetes and heart disease.

Vitamin Bone - 8%

Magnesium - 6%

Chromium - 6%

Calcium - 6%

Iron - 5%

Phosphoru - S5%

Vitamin A - 5%

Omega-3 Fats - 5%

Potassium5%

Choline - 5%

Protein - 5%

Vitamin B3 - 5%

Vitamin B6 - 4%

Vitamin E-- 4%

Black Beans, Cooked

Serving Size:

one/2 cup

Calories: oneone3

Fat: <one g

Saturated Fat: <one g

Cholesterol: 0 mg

Carbohydrate: 20 g

Protein: 8 g

Dietary Fiber: 8 g

Sodium: one mg

Thiamin: <one mg

Folic Acid: one28 mcg

Copper: <one mg

Iron: 2 g

Magnesium: 60 mg

Manganese: <one mg

Phosphorus: one20 mg

Potassium: 306 mg

See more at the Bean Institute.

http://beaninstitute.com

**Food Uses:**

Garden beans may be consumed green, before the pod matures as green, snap bean. Alternatively, allow the bean pod to mature and harvest them as dried beans. Green snap beans may be eaten either cooked or raw. Dry beans serve as a base for soups, stews, baked beans or any number of other ways.

**Harvesting:**

## Green Beans

Once the beans appear, you may eat them at any stage. Most gardeners wait until the beans are the diameter of a pencil. They should be firm and just before the bean seeds forming inside start to show. At this point, they will "snap" when broken in two. The oftener you pick the beans, the more they will produce. To harvest, grasp the joint where the bean joins the vine and pull with the other hand. For best flavor, cook right away but they will keep for a couple of days in the refrigerator.

## Dry Beans

Wait until the pods are dry. At this point, the bean vine will probably be dead, too. Pull the beans from the vines and spread them out in a cool, dry place for a few days. After a few days, the pods should split open easily. Strip out the beans and allow them to dry a few more days in a cool, dry place. Then put into bags, canisters, or other container and store until used in a cool dry area. The beans should keep several months if stored properly.

## Dry Beans Storage

Dried beans store for about one year in a sealed plastic bag. They will store much longer in an oxygen-deprived environment. Vacuum packaging them can extend their shelf life to ten years or more as long as air is absent from them while in storage. To reconstitute dried beans, soak in three cups of water per one pound of beans overnight. Rinse and simmer for two to four hours, until tender.

**Fresh Storage:**

Put unwashed fresh green beans in a sealed plastic bag or plastic container with a tight sealing lid. Put them in the crisper drawer of the refrigerator. They should keep well for about seven days. Rinse well before cooking.

**Freezing**

Frozen green beans are easy to prepare and will last up to a year in the freezer, so it is worth preserving some of the harvest if you have an excess.

**To freeze:**

Choose good, crisp beans without blemishes.

Most beans have a "string" that runs down the seam of the pod. Remove the string by using your thumbnail to break off the end of the bean and pull the "string" out of the seam. Once you have "stringed" the beans snap, or cut them in half if you want cut beans. Dont do anything if you want whole beans. Wash the beans and rinse them. The next step is to blanch the beans. First, prepare a large bowl of ice water. Boil about one gallon of water for each pound of beans and put the beans in the boiling water. Work in small batches if you are dealing with a large quantity of beans. Boil whole beans for four minutes, medium beans for three minutes and small cut beans for two minutes. The goal is not to cook the beans. Blanching stops the enzyme action inside the bean that causes loss of flavor, color and texture. Blanching sterilizes the surface of the bean, killing microorganisms. It also preserves nutrients and softens the beans, making them easier to pack into freezer containers or bags. Dont over-blanch them, or under blanch.

After you have blanched the beans, dump them in the ice water to cool them quickly. After they have cooled, drain in a colander and pack in freezer bags or containers. Label them, date them and put them in the freezer.

**Canning**

Canning green beans require more planning and equipment that freezing them. Nut many feel the taste of canned beans is superior to frozen one. Canned beans should also keep longer than frozen ones and not subject to spoilage if the power supply is interrupted.

You will need:

One pressure canner suitable for canning

Several quart or pint glass canning jars

Lids and rings adequate for the numbers of jars you have

Two pounds of fresh green beans for each quart jar you have. About one pound per pint

Water

Salt

Jar lifter

Before beginning, run your finger along the jar rim. If it is smooth, the jar should seal. If not, do not use it because it will not seal. This is not usually a problem with brand new jars, but jars that have been used several times can develop defects over time.

Steps in canning

one. Wash the beans, snip the ends. If you wish cut beans, snap them. Boil the beans in water for five minutes.

2. Simmer the jars in the canner; pour boiling water over the lids and rings to sterilize.

3. Pack the beans in the jars, leaving one-inch headspace. Add one teaspoon of salt to each jar and, using a stainless steel knife work out any air bubbles in the jar. Run a clean cloth along the edge of the jar rim to remove any debris. Put the lids on and tighten down with the screw rings finger tight. Put the jars in the canner.

4. Screw the lid on the pressure canner and turn on the heat. Allow ten pounds of pressure to build up, and then reduce the heat to maintain this pressure. Process quarts jars for twenty-five minutes, pints for twenty minutes. Adjust the time according to your altitude.

5. Remove from the heat and allow the pressure to reduce naturally. When the pressure has returned to normal, remove the lid and put the hot jars on a towel to allow to cool. Use a jar lifter to lift the jars to avoid scalding yourself. As the jars cool, you should hear the lids "clink" as they seal. After twenty-four hours, press down on the center of the lid. If the jar has sealed properly, it should be firm. You should not be able to press it down easily. Reprocess any jars that do not seal, or store in the refrigerator and consume within a week or so.

The hot water method of canning is not recommended for canning any type of home canned food. Always use a pressure canner for safety.

**Drying Green Beans**

It is possible to dry green beans. It was the only way to preserve them in pioneer times. They called them leather britches and they are quite easy to dry that way. Pick the beans at the "snap" stage. Cut into two to three inch lengths. Thread cotton kite string on a darning needle and stick through the end of one bean. Tie this bean in place by wrapping the end of the thread around it and securing it with a knot. Then just thread the remainder of the beans on the cord, one after another until you have a string about six or eight feet long. Tie the last bean on the same way you tied the first.

String the strand of beans up in a clean, dry area to dry. You could hang them in the attic or other area that is little used. After a few weeks, they will dry out to resemble green wooden chips. Either leave them hang or take them off the thread and store in a cool area in a glass or plastic jar with a screw lid. These should store for several weeks.

To cook, rinse them and put them in water to boil. Pour off the water after they begin to boil, and replace it. This removes any bitter taste and thoroughly cleans them. Pour on fresh water, season to taste and continue cooking them until they are tender.

## Cultivars:

Gardeners will find hundreds of varieties of garden beans on the market. This listing is by no means complete, but does list many of the top bean varieties.

### Bush Green Bean Cultivars

Jade Green Beans

Jade (60 days, BMV) produces very straight, dark-green round pods on vigorous plants. Jade produces later in the season than many other bush bean varieties. It is resistant to bean mosaic virus. It has light green seeds.

## Maxibel Bush Beans

Maxibel (50 days) is a dark green filet bean. It produces slender, seven-inch string-less pods. They will develop strings after the ideal harvesting time has passed. Pick every couple of days to avoid tough beans.

## Soliel Bush Bean Seeds

Soliel (60 days, OP) produces beautiful, uniformly slender filet-style beans, but with a gorgeous yellow color and great flavor. This variety has white seeds.

## Rolande Bush Beans

Rolande (50 days) is a fine green filet bean that produces slender, seven inch string-less pods, similar to Maxibel. Rolande stays tender at larger diameters than Maxibel.

Dragon Tongue (60 days, OP) produces pale yellow pods with mottled purple streaks on tall twenty four to thirty inch, vigorous plants. Versatile is an all-around bean that you can harvest young for green beans, or allow them to mature for shelling beans. Dragon Tongue has brown, mottled seeds.

## Provider

Provider (50 days, BMV, DM, and PM) is an easy-to-grow, adaptable green bean that performs well in cooler temperatures. Produces five to five and one-half inch round green pods. It is resistant to bean mosaic virus, downy mildew, and powdery mildew. It has purple seeds.

## Rocdor

Rocdor (52 days, A, BMV): Slender, yellow round pods, six to six and one-half inch long, on upright plants. Skinniest of the yellow wax beans. Warm yellow color makes them easy to spot for picking. This variety is resistant to anthracnose and bean mosaic virus. Black seeds germinate well in cooler temperatures.

## Royal Burgundy

Royal Burgundy (55-60 days) produces deep purple, five-inch pods that can be sliced into salads for color (the pods turn green when cooked). The purple color makes them easy to se. It has tan seeds.

## Tavera

Tavera (54 days, A, BMV) produces large yields of tender, slim four to five inch beans. Pick every other day to avoid tough beans. Taveray is resistant to anthracnose and bean mosaic virus. It has small white seeds.

## Blue Lake #47

Blue Lake #47 (60 days) this prolific variety is good fresh or frozen. It features six inch beans that are mostly straight, mildly sweet, ready in plants are less than two feet tall

## Green Beans Half-Runner

## Big Kahuna

Big Kahuna (57 days) this variety is available exclusively through the Burpee Seed Company, features giant-sized straight beans that reach eleven inches long, very crisp with a nutty and sweet flavor. The plants reach two feet tall.

## Early Bush Italian

Early Bush Italian - this heirloom green bean variety features classic flat pods, excellent flavor, beans average five inches long, string-less, freeze well, ready in 50 days. The plants rarely exceed eighteen inches tall.

## Purple Queen (52 days)

Purple Queen - this variety features straight purple pods that average seven inches long, turn green after cooking, beans are moderately nutty and tender. The plants average eighteen inches tall

Contender

Contender (55 days) one of the heaviest yielding green bean varieties, pods are slightly curved and average six inches long, very good flavor and tender texture, plants reach thirty inches tall.

Greencrop

Greencrop (50 days) this variety is an All-America Winner. The pods are flat like an Italian bean but thinner, pods are string-less and crisp, flavor is nutty and fresh.

Maxi Dwarf

Maxi Dwarf ( 50 days) The beans average eight inches long and are produced above the leaves for easy harvest, good flavor and texture. The pods are slightly curved at the end, heavy yields.

Fordhook Standard

Fordhook Standard (57 days) features slender and straight beans that average six t seven inches long. They are very sweet and crisp, plants average eighteen inches tall.

Blue Lake #274

Blue Lake #274 (58 days) beans are plump and average five to six inches long with white seeds and heavy yields. The beans freeze well. These plants average eighteen inches tall and are tender and nutty in flavor.

Triumphe De Farcy

Triumphe De Farcy (48 days) a French bush variety and early producer. The plants average one8" tall. The straight slender pods are crunchy and nutty. These beans are best when harvested between four and six inches long with heavy yields.

Eureka

Eureka (55 days) this unique variety features yellow beans that average 5"-6" long, slightly curved, plants are very short at only fifteen inches tall.

White Half Runner

White Half Runner (60 days) this variety features bright green beans that average four inch long, very tender and sweet with white seeds, heavy yields, plants average two feet tall

Jade

Jade (60 days) this green bean variety features dark green pods that are straight and string-less, very sweet and tender, pods average six inches long. The plants average twenty inches tall and is a good producer


## Pole Beans

Fortex (60 days, OP, A, BMV) produces early, high yields of extra-long pods — the longest pods of the pole beans. Harvest at seven inches for slender, filet-type green beans, or harvest larger beans up to eleven inches long. Fortex is string-less and tender even after seeds have started to swell. It has dark brown seeds.


Spanish Musica, a.k.a., Spanish Miralda (75 days) produces high yields of large, flat roma-type green beans on vigorous, six to ten foot vines. Optimal harvest at eight inches but pods stay tender up to ten inches. It has white seeds.


Rattlesnake (70-80 days) produces seven inch, round, green pods, streaked with purple — similar to Dragon Tongue bush beans. Vigorous, eight-foot vines. Rattlesnake has mottled, light brown seeds.

Kentucky Wonder (70 days OP,) is a classic heirloom green bean that produces flat, six to eight inch silvery-green pods on six to eight foot vines.

Goldmarie (75 days, OP) is a romano-type heirloom that produces high yields of flat, yellow, six inch pods on vigorous vines. It has white seeds.

Helda (60 days, OP, BMV) has large nine inch string-less, pale green pods, similar to Spanish Miralda. The vines are six to eight feet tall. Helda is resistant to bean mosaic virus.

Blue Lake Pole (75 days, OP, BMV) produces six to seven inch dark green, round pods, perfect for canning. Vigorous vines grow to seven feet. It has white seeds.

Kentucky Blue – (65 days) this variety features straight and string-less beans average seven inch long, heavy yields on plants that can reach nine feet fall. Kentucky Blue is a cross between Kentucky Wonder and Blue Lake

Blue Lake – (60 days)this variety features straight and string-less pods that average six inch long, moderately sweet and crisp, freezes well. plants can reach nine feet tall, also available as certified organic seeds

Kentucky Wonder – (65 days)plants can reach nine feet tall. This green bean variety features slightly curved pods that are string-less when young, pods are thick and meaty, good fresh or frozen. It is an heirloom variety also available as certified organic seed

Scarlett Runner –(70 days) this unique variety features bright red/orange flowers, beans are very slender and reach eight inch long, can be picked young for snap beans or shelled when fully mature. The plants can reach nine feet tall

Purple King - this unique variety features shiny purple beans that average 5"-6" long, beans turn green when cooked, and plants can reach 8 feet tall, ready in 75 days, beans are moderately sweet and tender

Asparagus Yardlong – (80 days) Unique variety with long and slender pods, best when picked before beans reach one8" long, nice nutty flavor, plants can reach 9 feet tall. These beans are best cooked quickly in stir-fry or sautéed

**Dry Beans**

It is possible to dry most bean varieties, but some varieties are better than others are for specific uses. Here is a partial list.

Adzuki

Appearance: - small, reddish brown

Flavor: - nutty, sweet

Culinary: - often used in Asian cuisine; particularly popular in Japanese cooking for confections

Cooking Time: - three-quarters to one hour

Baby Lima

Appearance: - flat-shaped, creamy white

Flavor: - rich, buttery

Culinary: - soups, stews and casseroles; or cooked with herbs and spices

Cooking Time: - one hour

Black Bean

Appearance: - small ovals with deep black skins; dark-cream-to-gray flesh

Flavor: - mild, sweet, earthy; soft texture

Culinary: - sometimes called turtle beans. Use them in classic Latin American, Caribbean and Southwestern cooking in soups, stews, sauces

Cooking Time: - one to one and a-half hours

Blackeye

Appearance: - kidney shape; white skin with small black eye, very fine wrinkles

Flavor: - scented aroma, creamy texture, distinctive flavor

Culinary: These originated in Africa. And are they are still very common there. They are also called cowpeas or black-eyed peas; cook rapidly with no pre-soaking needed

Try in stir-fried black eyes and beef or turkey and bean salad with apricot-ginger dressing.

Cooking Time: - one-half to one hour

Cranberry

Appearance: - small rounded beans, ivory color with red markings that disappear on cooking

Flavor: - creamy texture; subtle, nut-like taste

Culinary: - a favorite in northern Italian, Spanish and Portuguese cuisines

Cooking Time: - three-quarters to one hour

Dark Red Kidney

Appearance: - large, kidney-shaped, deep reddish-brown

Flavor: - robust, full-bodied, soft texture


Culinary: - often used in chili; popular in salads; paired with rice

Cooking Time: - one-half to two hours

Garbanzo

Appearance: - beige to pale yellow

Flavor: - nutlike taste, buttery texture

Try them in a grilled tuna and bean salad or make your own falafel.

Culinary: - called chickpeas; especially popular in Middle Eastern, Indian dishes — hummus, falafels, curries

Cooking Time: - one to one-half hours

Great Northern

Appearance: - flat, kidney-shaped, medium-sized, white

Flavor: - mild, delicate, take on flavors of other foods with which they're cooked

Culinary: popular in France in cassoulet (a white bean casserole); in U.S., traditionally prepared as Boston baked beans

Try them in pasta with beans and greens or sage-roasted pork tenderloin with beans.

Cooking Time: - three-quarters to one hour

Large Lima

Appearance: - flat shape, ivory color

Flavor: - smooth, creamy, sweet

Culinary: - sometimes called "butter beans"; used in American succotash. They are a good substitute for potatoes or rice; excellent in soups, casseroles

Try them in tomato butter bean bok Choy or white bean chili.

Cooking Time: - one to one and one-half hours

Light Red Kidney

Appearance: - large, kidney-shaped

Flavor: - robust, full-bodied flavor, soft texture

Culinary: - popular in Caribbean region, Portugal, Spain; most often used in chili, salads; often paired with rice

Try them in fettuccine, chicken and bean Alfred, or Asian bean and rice rolls.

Cooking Time: - one to one and one-half hours

Navy

Appearance: - small white ovals

Flavor: - mild flavor, powdery texture

Culinary: - called pea beans; most often used in pork and beans, baked beans; also used in soups and stews; are great pureed

Try them in navy bean oatmeal chocolate chip cookies or pasta e aioli.

Cooking Time: - one to two hours

Pink

Appearance: - small, pale-pink; turn reddish brown when cooked

Flavor: - rich, meaty with slightly powdery texture

Culinary: - related to kidney beans; often used in chili; a favorite in Old West (U.S.) recipes

Try them in pink beans with chicken breasts, oranges and walnuts or Cajun bean, corn and shrimp bisque.

Cooking Time: - one hour

Pinto

Appearance: - medium ovals; mottled beige and brown

Flavor: - earthy flavor, powdery texture

Culinary: - closely related to red kidney beans; when cooked, lose natural mottling on skins and turn brown; most often used in refried beans, Tex-Mex, Mexican dishes

Try them in pinto bean applesauce raisin cookies or southwest lasagna.

Cooking Time: - one-half to two hours

Small Red

Appearance: - dark red color, similar to red kidney but smaller

Flavor: - similar to red kidney

Culinary: - also called Mexican red beans; hold both shape and firmness when cooked; most often used in soups, salads, chili, Creole dishes

Try them in kidney bean and cheesy rice casserole or shrimp and red beans Creole.

Cooking Time: - one to one and a -half hours

## Cooking and Preparing:

Green Beans

To cook green beans, snip the ends and remove the string that usually runs along the seam, as in the instructions for freezing. Rinse and place the beans into a pan. Cover the beans with water and bring the water to a boil. Add onion, garlic and other seasonings, as desired. Once the beans boil, turn down the heat and allow to simmer until the beans soften. This can take five minutes or longer. Serve hot.

Dry Beans:

Cover the beans with water and season. Onions, garlic, bacon and pepper make good seasonings, but there are others. Bring to a boil, then turn the heat down and simmer the beans for one and a half to two hours. Crock-pots and other slow cookers are ideal to cook beans. Add potatoes, ham and onions to season them.

## Heirloom Varieties

Heirloom varieties are open pollinated varieties that have sometimes been handed down for generations in a family. These varieties have distinctive tastes and textures different from hybridized seed.

It you grow them and wish to save your own seed, allow the seeds you wish to harvest to mature fully on the vine. Try to save beans that look appear true to the form you are growing. Do not leave them hang too long, however. Once dry, pick them and spread the pods in a dry, cool place to dry further. After a few days, they should strip easily from the pods. Once stripped further drying them a few days can be beneficial. Store the bean seed in an airtight container in the freezer or the crisper drawer of the refrigerator.

The beans should stay true for many generations, though some variations may occur.

There are far too many varieties available to describe in this guide. Below there are companies listed with full descriptions of the beans and quantities available for purchase. Additional planting instructions for the individual varieties can also be found.

## Cooking and Preparing:

Green Beans

To cook green beans, snip the ends and remove the string that usually runs along the seam, as in the instructions for freezing. Rinse and place the beans into a pan. Cover the beans with water and bring the water to a boil. Add onion, garlic and other seasonings, as desired. Once the beans boil, turn down the heat. Simmer them until the beans soften. This can take five minutes or longer. Serve hot.

Dry Beans:

Cover the beans with water and season. Onions, garlic, bacon and pepper make good seasonings, but there are others. Bring to a boil, then turn the heat down and simmer the beans for one and a half to two hours. Crock-pots and other slow cookers are ideal to cook beans. Add potatoes, ham and onions to season them.

## Heirloom Varieties

Heirloom varieties are open-pollinated varieties that have sometimes been handed down for generations in a family. These varieties have distinctive tastes and textures different from hybridized seed.

It you grow them and wish to save your own seed, allow the seeds you wish to harvest to mature fully on the vine. Try to save beans that look appear true to the form you are growing. Do not leave them hang too long, however. Once dry, pick them and spread the pods in a dry, cool place to dry further. After a few days, they should strip easily from the pods. Once stripped further drying them a few days can be beneficial. Store the bean seed in an airtight container in the freezer or the crisper drawer of the refrigeration.

The beans should stay true for many generations, though some variations may occur.

There are far too many varieties available to describe in this guide. Below there are companies listed with full descriptions of the beans and quantities available for purchase. Additional planting instructions for the individual varieties can also be found.

**Heirloom Seed Available From:**

Heirloom Seed

Phone:

(859) 986-3204

Mailing Address:

Sustainable Mountain Agriculture Center

1033 Pilot Knob Cemetery Road

Berea, Kentucky 40403

Farm Address:

Sustainable Mountain Agriculture Center

1033 Pilot Knob Cemetery Road

Berea, Kentucky 40403

Baker Creek Heirloom Seed Co.

2278 Baker Creek Road

Mansfield, MO 65704

 Phone: (417) 924-8917

Fax: (417) 924-8887

email: seeds@rareseeds.com


Eden Brothers

34 Old Brevard Road

Asheville, NC 28806

Call Us: (828) 633 - 6338

email: service@edenbrothers.com

http://www.edenbrothers.com/store/


Victory Seed Company

P.O. Box 192 -

Molalla, Oregon 97038

(503) 829-3126 (voicemail line)

http://www.victoryseeds.com/


Heirloom Seeds

287 E. Finley Dr.

West Finley PA 15377

e-mail: mail@heirloomseeds.com

http://heirloomseeds.com/

**Seed Catalog List**

Amanda's Garden Native Perennial Nursery

Phone: 585-669-2275

amandasgarden@frontiernet.net

8410 Harper's Ferry Road

Springwater, NY 14560

http://www.amandasnativeplants.com/


http://www.ambergategardens.com/index.html

Ambergate Gardens

8730 County Road 43,

Chaska, MN 55318-9358.

(877) 211-9769. $2


Antonelli Brothers

407 Hecker Pass

Watsonville, CA 95076

Phone: 1-888-423-4664

Website: www.antonellibegonias.com

Email Contact: linda@antonellibegonias.com

Their specialty is the tuberous begonia, but they offer other plants too.


Bluestone Perennials, Inc.

7211 Middle Ridge Rd

Madison, OH 44057

1.800.852.5243

http://www.bluestoneperennials.com/

(800) 852-5243


Burgess Seed and Plant Co.

905 Four Seasons Road

Bloomington IL 61701

309-662-7761

www.eburgess.com

56 pages

Burgess offers an interesting mix of perennials, shrubs, trees, and vegetable seeds. There are also fruit and nut trees, roses, and strawberries.


Burpee

W. Atlee Burpee Company

Warminster PA 18974

1-800-888-1447

www.burpee.com

2007 updates for Burpee. They are introducing a new tomato variety,

a Burpee exclusive called Porterhouse Beefsteak. See the new varieties

for a short description of this one. They also have new impatiens, geranium, and potato introductions this year, among others. They have

expanded an already generously sized catalog. It doesn't look like

they have added any one thing in particular, but have generally added

new things into every category.


The W. Atlee Burpee Company is one of the leading seed companies

in the gardening industry. The catalog lists good selections of annual and

perennial flowers as well as vegetable seeds. Many, many tomatoes listed in

addition to sweet corn and squash.


Charley's Greenhouse

17979 State Road 536

Mount Vernon WA 98273-3269

1-800-322-4707

www.charleysgreenhouse.com

88 pages

If you love greenhouses, you will love this catalog. It has greenhouses of all types. Lean-to greenhouses, free standing one, small, portable greenhouses and large ones suitable for a small commercial grower. The catalog lists just about everything you need to grow plants, even if you don't have a greenhouse. Seed starter supplies, sprayers, irrigation equipment, composters, shredders, its all here.

CherryGal

Toll-Free: 888-752-0022

email: CherryGal@nc.rr.com

http://www.cherrygal.com/


Creek Hill Nursery

17 West Main Street

Leola, PA 17540

PH: 717-556-0000

Toll Free: 888-565-0050

http://www.creekhillnursery.com/


Dayton Nurseries, Inc.

3459 Cleveland-Massillon Rd.

Norton, OH 44203

330-825-3320

1-866-500-6605

http://www.daytonnursery.com/


Edmunds Roses

335 S High Street

Randolph, Wisconsin 53956

1-800-347-7609

www.edmundsroses.com

48 pages

45 pages of roses. Tea roses, miniature roses, old fashioned roses, just about any kind of rose you can think of. The last 3 pages are devoted to fertilizers, tools and insecticides you will need for your roses.


Everwilde Farms

Everwilde Farms, Inc.

PO Box 40

Sand Creek, WI 54765

Toll Free: 1 (888) 848-3837

Local: 1 (715) 658-0001

http://www.everwilde.com/


Farmers Seed and Nursery

Division of Plantron, Inc

818 NW 4th Street

Fairbault, MN 55021

1-850-7334-1623

www.farmerseed.com

40 pages

This catalog has a good selection of nursery stock including ornamental shrubs and trees. Fruit includes strawberries, blackberries and raspberries. Other types of fruit trees and vines, too. Nut trees, perennial plants and roses, also. There is a good selection of vegetable seed.

Farmtek

1440 Field of Dreams

Dyersville, IA 52040

1-800-327-6835

www.farmtek.com

Extensive offerings of greenhouse supplies, including conduit to use to build your own. It also has tarps, fencing, weather shield canopies of many types, lighting, fans and heating supplies. This is a general farm supply catalog with items of some interest to the gardener, as there are large greenhouses and smaller portable structures as well as gardening supplies.


Fleming's Flower Fields

 Lincoln, Nebraska

1-855-442-4488

1-559-920-1476

http://www.flemingsflowers.com/


Forest Farm

990 Tetherow Rd.

Williams, OR 97544-9599.

(541) 846-7269. $4

Phone Orders: (541)846-7269

Monday-Friday (8-4 PST)

Fax Orders: (541)846-6963

Email: plants@forestfarm.com

http://www.forestfarm.com/contact_us.php

Four Seasons Nursery

1706 Morrissey

Bloomington, IL 61704

www.4seasonsnurseries.com

48 pages

This catalog encompasses nursery plants of all types. Shrubs, perennials, and trees are included within its pages. Dwarf citris trees for the patio. It also includes fruit trees and berry plants.

Garden Crossings L.L.C.

4902 96th Ave.

Zeeland, MI 49464

Phone: (616) 875-6355

http://www.gardencrossings.com/

Gardeners Supply

128 Intervale Road

Burlington, VT 05401

1-800-427-3363

www.gardeners.com

This catalog focuses on organic gardening supplies. They have a wonderful selection of tomato towers. There are also containers for patio gardening, trelleses, kits to build raised beds and much more in this delightful catalog. There are many items suitalble as gifts for gardeners. You will also find growing supplies, seed starting supplies, fertilizers, organic pesticides and other gardening supplies.

George W. Park Seed Company

1 Parkton Ave

Greenwood, SC 29647-0001

1-800-845-3369

www.parkseed.com

146 pages

This bountiful catalog has extensive offerings of all categories of seeds -

herbs, vegetables, annual and perennial seeds. There is also a generous

offering of fruit and berry plants like grapes, blackberries and strawberries.

New this year is a selection of organic seeds. Park seed is one of the

premier seed catalogs that no gardener should be without.

Gilbert H. Wild

PO Box 338

Sarcoxie, MI 64862-0338

1-888-449-4537

www.gilberthwild.com

This grower has been in business since 1885. The catalog offers a large selection of daylilies, iris and peonies. They do have many other perennials.

Great Garden Plants,Inc.

P.O. Box 1511

Holland, MI 49422-1511

http://www.greatgardenplants.com/

Greenwood Nursery

636 Myers Cove Road

McMinnville, TN 37110

1-800-426-0958

http://www.greenwoodnursery.com/

Grower's Supply

1440 Field of Dreams Way

Dyersville, IA 52040

1-800-476-9715

www.growerssupply.com

This is the ultimate greenhouse supply catalog, supplying everything from

large commercial greenhouses to small, hobby houses. There are also cold

frames, hot beds, raised bed kits for gardens, arched bridges, fencing and netting. Greenhouse heaters, benches, growing supplies, chemicals and all

other greenhouse growing supplies.

Gurney's Seed and Nursery

PO Box 4178

Greendale, IN 47025-4178

513-354-1491

www.gurneys.com

66 Pages

Gurney's large format catalog offers large selections of vegetables, flowers, fruits and supplies for gardening. They also list trees, shrubs, roses, and nut trees. This is one of the older seed companies, they have been selling seeds for many years.

Harris Seeds

355 Paul Road

PO Box 24966

Rochester, NY 14624-0966

1-800-514-4441

www.harrisseeds.com

82 pages

Heavy selection of vegetable seeds, with a nice offering of flower seeds, too. They have almost 20 pages of gardening supplies like seed starting equipment, flats and carts.

Hidden Valley Nature Arts

36175 Alamar Mesa Drive

Hemet, California 92545

Phone: 951-926-7330

http://www.hiddenvalleyhibiscus.com/


High Country Gardens

2902 Rufina Street

Santa Fe, NM 87507-2929

Phone: 800-925-9387

Fax: 800-925-0097

Annuals

Bulbs

Perennials

Exotic Plants and Flowers

Flower, Vegetable and Wildflower Seeds

Garden Supplies, Tools and Power Equipment

Gifts and Decorative Accessories

Ground Covers, Shrubs, Trees, and Vines

Fertilizer, Weed & Pest Control Products

Magazines and Books

Ornamental Grasses and Plants

Roses

Other

High Country Gardens specializes in waterwise ("xeric") perennials and other plants that need very little or no extra water once established. With the widespread awareness of green, environmentally conscious practices, the use of drought tolerant plants has now spread from the high desert gardens of the Southwest to the entire nation. We have spent years offering and developing unusual garden-tested perennials, bulbs, cacti, succulents, grasses, and shrubs that ship right from our greenhouses to your landscape. The fragrant and colorful blossoms and foliage on many of our flowering xeriscape plants, such as Lavender, Penstemon, and Agastache, attract hummingbirds and butterflies.

Website: www.highcountrygardens.com

Click Here to Subscribe to our Newsletter

Email Contact: plants@highcountrygardens.com


HPS - Horticultural Products and Services

334 West Stroud Street

Randolph WI 53956

130 pages

1-800-322-7288

www.hpsseed.com

This catalog caters to the commercial market or greenhouse grower, though

the gardener who grows larger quantities of plants may find it useful, too.

Flower plugs, seeds for flowers and vegetables, and grower supplies. The

flower seeds include both annual and perennial. Most are available in both large, commercial quantities and smaller amounts suitable for the

home grower. Grower supplies include seed starter units, flats and inserts,

greenhouse supplies, fertilizers and insecticides.

John Scheepers Kitchen Garden Seeds

23 Tulip Drive

PO Box 838

Bantam, CT 06750-0638

1-860-567-6086

www.kitchengardenseeds.com

52 pages

This catalog focuses on vegetables and herbs. It has unusual and old time varieties as well as some of the favorites. The salad green selection of seeds is excellent. There are also Asian greens and sprouting seeds. There are some flower seeds, mostly annual fragrant and cutting flowers. This is a nice catalog with some unusual seed offerings.

Johnny's Selected Seeds

955 Benton Ave.

Winslow, ME 04901

Phone: 877-564-6697

Fax: 800-738-6314

Annuals

Bulbs

Perennials

Flower, Vegetable and Wildflower Seeds

Fruit Trees and Berries

Garden Supplies, Tools and Power Equipment

Gifts and Decorative Accessories

Greenhouses and Indoor Gardening Supplies

Ground Covers, Shrubs, Trees, and Vines

Herbs and Vegetables

Irrigation Supplies and Equipment

Fertilizer, Weed & Pest Control Products

Magazines and Books

Ornamental Grasses and Plants

Johnny's Selected Seeds is a mail-order seed producer and merchant located in Albion and Winslow, Maine, USA. The company was established in 1973 by our Founder and Chairman Rob Johnston, Jr. Johnny's prides itself on its superior product, research, technical information, and service for home gardeners and commercial growers.

Our products include vegetable seeds, medicinal and culinary herb seeds, and flower seeds. We also offer unique, high quality gardening tools and supplies. Our Export Department ships seeds internationally, and welcomes your inquiry. Of course, we also ship throughout the United States. We sell both retail and wholesale, small to large quantities.

Website: Johnnyseeds.com

Click Here to Subscribe to our Newsletter

Email Contact: homegarden@johnnyseeds.com


J. W. Jung Seed Company

335 South High Street

Randolph, WI 53957-0001

1-800-247-5864

www.jungseed.com

115 Pages

Jung sells a very interesting mix of fruit trees and plants, shrubs and

trees, vegetable and flower seed, and gardening supplies. Perennial plants,

flower bulbs, lilies and roses are included in the offerings. This is a

"must have" catalog for the gardener.


Kelley Nurseries

Division of Plantron

410 8th Ave NW

Faribault, MN 55021

www.kelleynurseries.com

56 pages

This is strictly a nursery catalog with good selections of perennials, ground covers, roses,

and ornamental grasses. Sections of water plants and nut trees also listed. Strong sections of ornamental trees, shrubs and fruit plants.

VanBourgondien

PO Box 2000

Virginia Beach, VA 23450

1-800-622-9959

www.dutchbulbs.com

68 pages.

This catalog is full of plant bulbs and perennial plants. They have a very large selection of dahlias. Also tropical bulbs, cannas, peonies, daylilies, and lilies. The perennial selection is excellent.


Magnolia Gardens

1980 Bowler Road

Waller, TX 77484

936-931-9927

http://magnoliagardensnursery.com/


Michigan Bulb Company

Customer Service

P.O. Box 4180

Lawrenceburg, IN 47025-4180

Phone: (812) 260-2148

http://www.michiganbulb.com/

McClure & Zimmerman

335 South High Street

Randolph, WI 53956

1-800-883-6998

www.mzbulb.com

32 pages

Two catalogs per year, a spring one with the spring bulb offerings and a second one in the autumn for the fall selections. Spring offerings include begonias, caladiums, cannas, daylilies, iris, and much more. Very large selection of bulbs and tubers.

Musser Forests

Dept S-07M

1880 Route 119 Highway N

Indiana PA 15701-7341

1-800-643-8319

www.musserforest.com

48 Pages

This is a nursery catalog for the landowner or nursery owner. The offerings are trees and shrubs, mostly in smaller sizes suitable for planting in nursery rows or containers. Some are suitable for planting in the garden. Most are offered in larger quantities of 5, 10, or more. Selections

include evergreen trees, deciduous trees, shrubs, groundcovers, and perennial plants.

Nature Hills Nursery, Inc.

3334 North 88th Plaza

Omaha, NE 68134

Phone: 888-864-7663

Fax: 866-550-9556

Annuals

Bulbs

Perennials

Exotic Plants and Flowers

Flower, Vegetable and Wildflower Seeds

Fruit Trees and Berries

Garden Supplies, Tools and Power Equipment

Gifts and Decorative Accessories

Greenhouses and Indoor Gardening Supplies

Ground Covers, Shrubs, Trees, and Vines

Herbs and Vegetables

Irrigation Supplies and Equipment

Fertilizer, Weed & Pest Control Products

Magazines and Books

Ornamental Grasses and Plants

Roses

Other

Nature Hills Nursery, Inc. was originally founded in 2001 as a conifer and deciduous tree nursery. Nature Hills Nursery started as a local tree nursery serving a limited geographic area. Our company has evolved and responded to our customers' demand of quality nursery products. We continue to improve our on-line capabilities and expand our product offerings.

Website: www.naturehills.com

Email Contact: info@NatureHills.com


Niche Gardens

1111 Dawson Rd

Chapel Hill, NC 27516

(919) 967-0078.

http://www.nichegardens.com/


North Creek Nurseries - Corporate Office

388 North Creek Road

Landenberg, PA 19350

Tel.: 610-255-0100

Toll Free: 877-ECO-PLUG

http://www.northcreeknurseries.com/


Oakland Nurseries

http://oaklandnursery.com/

The Garden Centers below are affiliated with Oakland Nurseries

Columbus Garden Center

1156 Oakland Park Avenue

Columbus, OH 43224-3317

Phone: 614-268-3511

Fax: 614-784-7700

Delaware Garden Center
25 Kilbourne Road
Delaware, OH 43015
Phone: 740-548-6633
Fax: 740-363-2091

Dublin Garden Center
4261 West Dublin-Granville Road
Dublin, Ohio 43017
Phone: 614-874-2400
Fax: 614-874-2420

New Albany Garden Center
5211 Johnstown Road
New Albany, Ohio 43054
Phone: 614-917-1020
Fax: 614-917-1023

Outsidepride.com, Inc.
915 N. Main
Independence, OR 97351
800-670-4192
http://www.outsidepride.com/

Perennial Pleasures Nursery

P.O. Box 147

E. Hardwick

VT 05836.

(802) 472-5104. $3

http://perennialpleasures.net/


Perryhill Nurseries Ltd

Edenbridge Road

Hartfield

East Sussex

TN7 4JP

Phone:01892 770377

Fax: 01892 770929

Email: sales@perryhillNurseries.co.uk

http://www.perryhillnurseries.co.uk/locate/


Pinetree Garden Seeds

PO Box 300

New Gloucester, ME 04260

1-926-3400

www.superseeds.com

115 pages

The catalog claims over 900 varieties of seeds, bulbs, tubers, garden books and products. The listings are pretty extensive with the emphasis on vegetable seeds. There are sections for ethnic vegetables like Asian, Italian, and Latin American. The flower offerings include both annual and perennial flower seeds. The garden book section is impressive, boasting 14 pages of gardening related books. Several pages of garden supplies, there is even a Garden-opoly game.

Plant Delights Nursery, Inc.

9241 Sauls Road

Raleigh, NC 27603

Phone: 919.772.4794

http://www.plantdelights.com/


Prairie Moon Nursery

32115 Prairie Lane

Winona, MN  55987

Toll Free: (866) 417-8156

http://www.prairiemoon.com


Restoration Seeds

1133 Old Highway 99 S.

Ashland, OR 97520

1-541-201-2688

http://www.restorationseeds.com/

Roots and Rhizomes

PO Box 9

Randolph, WI 53956-0009

1-800-374-5035

www.rootsrhizomes.com

60 pages

Specializing in choice daylilies, siberian iris, hostas, and perennials. If you like any of those plants, this beautiful catalog will have something you want. Twenty pages of daylilies are at the beginning of the catalog and they are followed by hostas, iris and much more. They also have a large selection of other perennials like astilbe, aster, coriopsis, and geraniums.


Seeds of Change

PO Box 15700

Santa Fe NM 87592-1500

1-888-762-7333

www.seedsofchange.com

84 pages

This catalog is for vegetable lovers as it is mostly devoted to them, and

all seeds sold by this company are certified organic. There

is a section of flower seeds, but veggies take center stage. There is a full

page of garlic varieties! Gourmet greens and herbs are in good supply, too.

There is also a good selection of gardening books and gardening supplies.

Select Seeds

180 Stickney Hill Road

Union, CT 06076

1-860-684-9310

www.selectseeds.com

67 Pages

If you are looking for something a bit out of the mainstream or "different" then Select Seeds is the catalog you are looking for. Most of the seeds and plants offered are not found in the major outlets. Special sections for fragrant and old fashioned plants are featured. This catalog is a must for the home gardener looking for a flower garden that stands out a bit.

Seymours Selected Seeds

334 West Stroud Street

Randolph, WI 53596

1-800-353-9516

www.seymourseedusa.com

46 pages

This small catalog is packed with a full selection of annual and perennial flowers for the home gardner. Many unusual varieties and old time favorites. There is also a nice selection of bulbs and perennial plants.

Sooner Plant Farm, Inc

25976 S. 524 Rd.

Park Hill, OK 74451

Tel.: (918)453-077


Southern Exposure Seed Exchange

PO Box 460

Mineral, VA 23117

Phone: 540-894-9480

Fax: 540-894-9481

Annuals

Bulbs

Perennials

Exotic Plants and Flowers

Flower, Vegetable and Wildflower Seeds

Fruit Trees and Berries

Garden Supplies, Tools and Power Equipment

Gifts and Decorative Accessories

Ground Covers, Shrubs, Trees, and Vines

Herbs and Vegetables

Irrigation Supplies and Equipment

Fertilizer, Weed & Pest Control Products

Magazines and Books

Ornamental Grasses and Plants

Other

We are a wonderful source for vegetables selected in a day where taste and local adaptability were the primary factors. We have an extensive line of heirloom and other open pollinated seeds and seed saving supplies. Many of our varieties are certified organic. We also carry a wide variety of garlic and perennial onion bulbs and medicinal herb rootstock. We are a source for naturally colored cotton seeds. Many of our products are Certified Organic.

Website: www.southernexposure.com

Email Contact: gardens@southernexposure.com


SpringHill

110 West Elm St.

Tipp City, OH 45371

1-513-354-1509

www.springhillnursery.com

52 pages

This catalog is loaded with perennials of all kinds. It has ground covers, grasses, clematis and much more. There is even a page of Bonsai trees. There is a nice rose section, ornamemtal trees and shrubs.


Stark Bro's

P.O. Box 1800

Louisiana, MO 63353

Email: info@starkbros.com

Phone: 800.325.4180

http://www.starkbros.com/

Swallowtail Garden Seeds

122 Calistoga Road, #178

Santa Rosa, CA 95409

Phone: Toll Free 1-877-489-7333

707-538-3585

http://www.swallowtailgardenseeds.com/


Siskiyou Rare Plant Nursery

2825 Cummings Rd.

Medford, OR 97501

(541) 772-6846. $3

http://siskiyourareplantnursery.com/


Tater-Mater Seeds

PO Box 16085

Seattle, WA 98116

http://tatermaterseeds.com/shop/


Territorial Seed Company

PO Box 158

Cottate Grove, OR 97424

1-541-942-9547

www.territorialseed.com

160 page catalog

This is a good catalog for market gardeners. Territoral has a big selection

of vegetables. There are a lot of different varieties of beans, with 25 pound bags available many varieties. Sweet and popcorn also well represented. Many varieties of lettuce also listed. Melons, peppers, peas, pumpkins and squash, along with boatloads of tomatoes. They also have a large selecion of annual flowers, available in larger quantities, so small greenhouse growers would find this catalog helpful. There are approximately 30 varieties of sunflowers, and lots of herbs. There is a good selection of growing supplies, including several types of spun bond fabric row covers. You will find a pretty good selection of organic growing aids in here also.Also a small selection of honey bee supplies, including a mason bee starter kit.

Thompson and Morgan

220 Faraday Ave

Jackson NJ 08527

1-800-274-7333

www.thompsonandmorgan.com

200 pages of pure joy! Thompson and Morgan is one of the most complete seed catalogs available to the home gardener. You will find something of everything including the most popular annual and perennial flowers, vegetables and herbs, tree seeds and houseplants. There are hard to find varieties, standard varieties and some downright odd and unusual varieties.

This catalog focuses on seeds, so you won't find many gardening supplies.

Thompson and Morgan is one seed catalog the serious gardener shouldn't be

without.


Totally Tomatoes

334 West Stroud Street

Randolph, WI 53956

1-800-345-5977

www.totallytomato.com

41 pages of nothing but tomatoes. They have the standard varieties available everywhere like Burpee Big Boy and Park Whopper. But there are many hard to find varieties like Aunt Ruby's German Green, Dixie Golden Giant and Bloody Butcher. They also have a good selection of peppers (16 pages), salad greens and cucumbers. Nice catalog and very interesting.


Vermont Bean Seed Company

334 W Stroud Street

Randolph, WI 53956

800-349-1071

www.vermontbean.com

79 page catalog.

These folks really do have the beans, sixteen pages of them. The catalog is chuck full of other stuff, too. Vegetable seeds are in good supply as well

as some flower seeds and herbs. They also sell vegetable and flower plants.

Garden supplies include a nice selection of organic garden aids,and seed

starting supplies.

Viette, Andre, Farm & Nursery,

Rt. 1, Box 16,

Fishersville, VA 22939.

(703) 943-2315. $3

http://www.viette.com/

Wayside Gardens

1 Garden Lane

Hodges, SC 29695-0001

1-800-845-1124

www.waysidegardens.com

164 pages

Wayside Gardens is an exclusively nursery stock catalog with extensive offerings of perennials, roses, shrubbery and ornamental trees. Many offerings are exclusive to them, or hard to find plants. This is the catalog for the discriminating gardener who is looking for the new, unusual, or unique.

Wildseed Farms

425 Wildflower Hills

PO Box 3000

Fredericksburg TX 78624-3000

1-800-848-0078

www.wildseedfarms.com

50 Pages

The catalog contains extensive instructions about how to establish wildflower stands. There are regional wildflower mixes as well as selections of individual wildflowers. Seeds are available in small gardener sized packets as well as bulk quantities suitable for large plantings. There is also a section of native grasses.

**Mossy Feet Books Catalog**

**To Get Your Free Copy of the Mossy Feet Books Catalogue, Go to Mossy Feet Books and click the catalog link.**

**Gardening Books**

*Abe's Guide to Growing the Tomato*

*The Solar Garden*

*Abe's Guide To The Peony*

*Abe's Guide to The Lanceleaf Coreopsis*

*Abe's Guide To The Threadleaf Coreopsis*

*Abe's Guide To The Creeping Phlox*

*Abe's Guide To The Hibiscus*

*Abe's Guide to Wall Germander*

*Abe's Guide To The Bearded Iris*

*Abe's Guide to the Chrysanthemum*

*Abe's Guide to the Fall Garden*

*Abe's Guide To Perennial Candytuft*

*Abe's Guide to Making Compost*

*Abe's Guide to Botany*

*Abe's Guide To Plant Stems*

*Abe's Guide to Buddleia*

*Abe's Guide to Leaves*

*Abe's Guide to Blanket Flower*

*Abe's Guide to Blackberry Lily*

*Abe's Guide to Flowers*

*Abe's Guide to Perennial Balloon Flower*

*Abe's Guide to Perennial Alyssum*

*Brilliant yellow blossoms and evergreen foliage make perennial alyssum a must for every perennial garden.*

*Abe's Guide to the Plant Root*

*The Complete Guide to the Plant Seeds*

*The Guide to Robotic Vacuum Cleaners*

*Abe's Guide to September/October Wildflowers*

*Abe's Guide to August Wildflowers*

*Abe's Guide to July Wildflowers*

*Abe's Guide to June Wildflowers*

*Abe's Guide to May Wildflowers*

*Abe's Guide to April Wildflowers*

*Abe's Guide to Growing Marigolds*

*Abe's Guide to Full Sun Perennials*


**Fantasy Books**

*Fading Photographs*

*Calls After Midnight*

*The Pirate King*

*Bearl's First Test*

*Heir of the Pirate King*

*Rise of the Pirate King*

*Tarque's Search*

*The Fall of Acerland*

*Legend of the Wizard Tarque*

*Covenant's Peril*

*Tale of the Crystal Eye*

*Flea Market Tales – Collection 1*

*The Wine Goblet*

*Box of Secrets*

*Lament of Arii*

*Glade of Death*

*Before the Storm*

*Gault*

*The Order of Solaun*

*Radio Memories*

*Seven Day Clock*

*Revealed by the Light*

*Zerena*

*Restoration*

*Time of Troubles*

*War of the Crystal*

*The Oasis*

*Pillars of Borr*

*Turmoil*

*Awakening*

*Demon Soul*

*Barn of Fear*

*Ten Tales for the Campfire*

*Five Tales for the Campfire – Volume Two*

*Halloween Party*

*The Dinner Bell Rings at Midnight*

*The Sinkhole*

*The Woman in the Wind*

*Tale of the White Rock*

*Field of Snakes*

*What's in the Cooler, Mister?*

*The Covenant*

*Five Tales for the Campfire*

*Promise of the White Rock*

*The Skull Garden*

*The Hungry House*

*Appointment*

*The Rise of Gwaum*

*Pets*

*Footsteps*

**Gandy Rand – Erotic**

*Short Stories and Collections*

*Double Trouble*

*Motorcycle Ride*

*Mrs. Boswell*

*Sales Call*

*Slow Day*

*Five Erotic Stories Collection 1*

*Mile High Club*

*Euchre Game*

*Masquerade Ball*

*Candy Store*

*Special Delivery*

*Five Erotic Stories Collection 2*

*Five Erotic Stories Complete Collection*

## Humor Books

*Stroke and Counterstroke*

*Five Stories From the Liar's Bench*

*Screams in the Night*

*Old Cameras Never Die*

*Whose Kidneys Are These, Anyway?*

*Practical Joke*

*Ad Space*

*Ten Funny Stories Complete Collection*

*Five Funny Stories – Volume II*

*Dog Ballooning*

*Holey Boat*

*Bring Your Pet to Work Day*

*An Ode to the Big Toe*

*Toe Tag*

*Five Funny Stories*

*Hole to China*

*One Fine Morning on Mulberry Lane*

*Perfect Afternoon*

*Truffle Shop Tale*

*The Adventures of Toby and Wilbur Complete Short Story Collection*

*Toby and Wilbur Bear– Legend of the Christmas Train*

*Toby and Wilbur and the Legend of the Trestletown Ghost*

*Toby and Wilber - The Great Kite Caper*

*Toby and Wilbur Bear – 3, 2, 1, Blastoff*

*Toby and Wilbur Bear – The Great Bear Race*

*Rich Woman's Dog*

*Bernie Fuller though life as a rich woman's dog would be a hoot.*

*Toby and Wilbur Bear – The Amazing Hovercraft Adventure*

*Toby and Wilbur – The Second Day*

*Toby and Wilbur – The Beginning Begins*


## Science Fiction Books

*Solar Power Primer*

*Alternative Energy Sources*

*Five Science Fiction Short Stories - Volume II*

*Ten Science Fiction Short Stories*

*Signals*

*Spores*

*Mind Games*

*Biology Experiment*

*The Database*

*Secretary General*

*Five Science Fiction Short Stories*

*Ad Campaign*

*The Smoke*

*The Elixir*

*Unacceptable Use of Resources*

*Down the Barrel of a Gun*

Back to Garden Bean Index

## Semi – Autobiographical Books

*Ten Ricky Huening Stories*

*Five Ricky Huening Stories – Collection II*

*1963*

*People Are Like Peanuts*

*Clay Rockets*

*Cookie*

*The Crick*

*Five Ricky Huening Stories – Collection I*

*Hauling Out the Trash*

*The Time Machine*

*The Chicken House*

*The Magic Swing*

*The Shoe Fence*

## Travel Books

*The Hawaiian Chronicles – Our Hawaiian Cruise Adventures*

*The Alaska Chronicles – Our Alaskan Cruise Adventure*

*Indiana State Park Series*

*A Visit to Pokagon State Park, Indiana*

*A Visit to the Falls of the Ohio*

*A Visit to the Land of Lincoln, Indiana*

*A Visit to Harmonie State Park, Indiana*

*A Visit to Brown County State Park*

*A Visit to Spring Mill State Park*

## Two New Series Debut Late 2015

*Travels Through Indiana History – Indiana History Daytrips*

*Indiana History Markers, Sites, Museums and More*

*A Daily Historical Fact Collection about Indiana*

*Indiana Bicentennial History Series*

*Indiana History Day in History Series – 2015 Edition*

*American History A Year at A Time – 2015 Edition*

*American History A Day at A Time – December 2015 Edition*

*American History A Day at A Time – November 2015 Edition*

*American History A Day at A Time – October 2015 Edition*

*American History A Day at A Time – September 2015 Edition*

*American History A Day at A Time – August 2015 Edition*

*American History A Day at A Time – July 2015 Edition*

*American History A Day at A Time – June 2015 Edition*

*American History A Day at A Time – May 2015 Edition*

*American History A Day at A Time – April  2015 Edition*

## Sample Chapter

## The Hawaiian Chronicles – Our Hawaiian Adventures

## Episode I - The Journey Begins

To celebrate our 25th wedding anniversary the wife and I ventured to our 50th state. Many hours of planning and deliberation went into this journey. Our first debates centered on the method of transportation. I wanted to drive while the wife felt an airplane might be better. Much discussion centered on this controversy, and I am chagrined to admit I finally had to relent. Hours of research led me to believe that there is no highway to Hawaii, a serious omission on the part of our road builders. No road, no car! The wife was right, we had to fly.

So now that we had determined our mode of travel, what to do upon arrival? The wife wanted to sightsee! You know, actually drive around and look at things! Just like a couple of tourists. My idea was to hang out at the beach and look cool, just like they do on Baywatch. The wife made some snide remarks about my unique physique. The remarks intimated that it was not conducive to looking cool on the beach, which led to more discussions. Our negotiations soon centered on a cruise or a dogsled tour. The wife seemed to think that there weren't any dogsleds on Hawaii, so the Hawaiian Cruise won out.

We would tour the Hawaiian Islands aboard the ship SS Independence of the American Cruise Lines. The tour would include four islands and five ports in seven days. Beginning on Maui in the port of Kahalui on Sunday the ship would proceed to the port of Hilo on the island of Hawaii, the Big Island. We would spend Monday in Hilo. It would then proceed to the Kona Coast port of Kailua on Tuesday. Wednesday and Thursday, we would spend on the island of Oahu in the port of Honolulu. Friday's destination would be Nawilili on the island of Kauai. Saturday we would return to Maui

for the flight home.

The AAA travel agency in Columbus, Indiana handled our travel arrangements. Our itinerary included:

Cincinnati

Ohio

Dallas

Texas

Los Angeles

California

Honolulu

Hawaii

Kahalui

Packing and other preparatory arrangements were a nightmare. The wife wanted to pack scads of clothing. I said, hell, everyone in Hawaii walks around in swimming trunks and flip-flops, we don't need any clothes. She said I been to too many Jimmy Buffet concerts, which led to more discussions. Which I lost. Again. In the weeks before departure, the wife was in a frenzy of activity - shopping and picking out clothes to take. There were clothes hanging all over the house. They hung on doors, chairs, and chandeliers. Shoot, I went to sleep watching a basketball game and awoke to find six pairs of pants and some shirts hanging from my big toe. On the day of departure, we had twenty-five suitcases, six duffels, three backpacks, her purse and my wallet. I said this seemed a little extreme as we only had two backs, how could we use three backpacks. I actually won this point! EEEhah!

The day of our departure finally arrived on February 17, 2001. Our initial flight was out of Cincinnati, Ohio on Comair Flight 6009 to Dallas, Texas at 7:00 AM. Anyone that flies a lot probably hates it. However, this was only my second flight by commercial airline and I thoroughly enjoyed the experience. We have done a fair amount of traveling, but always by car. The take off was smooth, the sunrise above the clouds just spectacular. I am amazed at how hard the flight attendants work rolling the cart up and down the aisle - always with a smile. We arrived above Dallas about 9:30, landing at 9:45. This is, as all times will be for the flight out, Indiana Time. Dallas looks nice from the air. There must have been heavy rains as the rivers and streams looked flooded. We breakfasted at the airport, and then departed Dallas at 11:25 AM for Los Angeles on Delta Flight 2119. I had a window seat so I had a good view of the landscape underneath until we got to the Rockies. Since clouds now obscured the view, we passed the time reading.

Arrival in LA was around 2:30 PM. Here we had a rather lengthy layover so we ate, read, and slept. We finally boarded the plane for Hawaii at 5:45 PM. Delta Flight 1579 left LA at 6:15 PM for Honolulu, Hawaii. The view of the receding California coast was the last thing we would see for a while, as the sky over the Pacific was mostly cloudy. Seeing the mainland slip away was both exciting and scary.

When the plane began its descent to the islands, it was about 11:30 PM Indiana time. This is about 6:30 PM Hawaii time, so it was still daylight. We passed over the island of Oahu and started our approach to Honolulu International Airport. Honolulu is impressive from the air at night. The city is lit up above the sparkling Pacific waters. The volcanic mountains constitute a striking backdrop. It is a beautiful sight.

Although we were flying on the same plane from Honolulu to Kahului, we had to leave the plane so they could clean it. I told the flight attendants that the wife enjoyed cleaning. Would the consider a discount on the far if she vacuumed while I finished my nap? While the attendant considered this request, my shin developed a rather sharp pain. Needles to say, we left the plane. The flight crew noticed my limp.

We departed Honolulu for Kahului at about 1:00 AM. It was completely dark now, so we could see nothing of the island below us except lights. All our flights that day had been smooth, so the flight from Honolulu to Kahluiu was memorable for its uniqueness. The plane passed over two mountain ranges, and I swear the plane hit every mountain in them both. Moreover, they didn't fully pressurize the plane's cabin. My head felt like an over inflated basketball on the way up, and like the inside of a flushed toilet on the way down.

We landed at Kahului at 1:30 AM (Indiana Time) - 8:30 PM Hawaii time. Representatives of the American Hawaiian

Cruise line met us at the airport. They collected our luggage, which by this time was in much better shape than we were. They herded us on a bus and took us to the port for check-in. Here another representative of the Line greeted us. By this time, my head felt like someone had stuck it in a jug, sucked out all the air, and then smashed the jug with a hammer. OOOh the joys of air travel. By 2:00 AM, nineteen hours after leaving winter in Indiana, we were in the tropics! The Cruise Line had a special lunch prepared for arrivals. We ate, found our way back to our stateroom somehow, and immediately fell asleep. Welcome to Hawaii!

**NOTE:** *This trip occurred in 2001. Sadly, the American Cruise Lines has gone out of business and the SS Independence to the scrap heap.*

16825473R00049

Printed in Great Britain
by Amazon